Ask for What You Want
AND GET IT!

by

DR. GILDA CARLE

Published in New York by
InterChange Communications Training, Inc.

Copyright © 2016 InterChange Communications
Training, Inc.

Gilda-Gram® is a registered trademark owned by
InterChange Communications Training, Inc.

ISBN-13: 978-1-881829-11-9

Library of Congress Control Number: 2015904244

Printed in the United States

For more information visit
www.DrGilda.com

ACKNOWLEDGMENTS

Thank you to all who have so generously contributed
your true stories to help others who are reading this
book. Without your giving, there would be less
healthful living!
--Dr. Gilda

<u>Gilda-Gram®</u>

**You can get whatever you want—
as long as you believe you DESERVE it
because you EARNED it!**

CONTENTS

CHAPTER 1

WHO WANTS, WHO GETS?

As I write this, I keep hearing the words to that once popular rap song, "Tell me what you want, what you really, really want. Tell me what you want, what you really, really want." The words make me wonder: If people don't get what they want, is it because they just don't *tell* someone what they really, really want? Or, is it because they don't really, really *know* what they want? Or, maybe, is it because they don't truly *want* what they *say* they want?

From my counseling and coaching on Skype throughout the world (on www.DrGilda.com), and the clients who come to see me, I have found that many people have lingering issues about some*thing* or some*one* they wanted, yet were never able to get. Most of us suffer terrible disappointment when we don't get what we want. We retrace our steps to analyze what *really* happened, we obsess with "If only's," and we beat up on ourselves with "woulda-coulda-shoulda's." Yet, with all our anguish, we usually don't learn what needs to be changed for the future, to prevent the same thing from recurring. If you're reading this and experiencing some remorse right now about not getting something or someone you wanted badly, take a deep breath and relax. Finally, your disappointment is over. Follow the Dr. Gilda plan to Get What You Want, as described in this book, and you will achieve anything and everything you desire. Actually, I developed these techniques for myself—so I'm sure they work.

Remember Betty and Veronica from the Archie comics? Veronica was the "It Girl" who enticed Archie simply by believing she *deserved* to have him as her boyfriend. Veronica was what I call a "Will-Be Winner," always knowing that she *will be* winning exactly what she set her mark on.

Will-Be Winners are in control of their lives. If they come upon hard times, they use their experience as lessons for their next attempts at success. They are directed by their goals, despite others' criticism. In winter, instead of cursing the cold, they bundle up and go skiing!

Betty was the complete opposite. Although she continued to pine for Archie, she always lost out to Veronica. In one of their comic strips, even when Archie asked her to be his prom date, because she didn't believe she *deserved* his attentions, she dismissed his invitation as a joke.

Betty was what I call a "Wanna-Be Loser," always *wanting to be* someone else, like becoming a replica of Veronica. Since Betty never acknowledged her own abilities and strengths, she would never be able to pursue them.

Wanna-Be Losers lack self-esteem. They want to be like the "It Person" who appears to "have it all." But instead of striving and thriving on their own, they attempt to mimic others. Then, when they don't succeed—because copies are *never* as good as the real thing—they bemoan their sorry state. In winter, all they do is curse the cold, but remain where they are, shivering, instead of taking action to make themselves warm.

Unfortunately, there are a lot of Bettys around. Celebrity worshipers who lack substantial lives of their own are among them. In fact, "Celebrity Worship Syndrome," as one study names it, threatens to take over the lives of one in three people, according to psychiatrist Dr. James Houran, research team leader. The need to identify with others could also include those desperate to "keep up with the Joneses."

Marilyn fell into this category. When her girlfriend, Alice, introduced her new boyfriend to her, Marilyn immediately gave him a bunch of her business cards to distribute to all his friends. She didn't even know this guy, yet she told him she *needed* a boyfriend.

As soon as she left, Alice's guy dumped the cards in the trash, shaking his head about the desperation of this needy chick. He had picked up Marilyn's belief that she didn't *deserve* to get a guy on her own, and she was willing to indiscriminately seek anyone who would do her bidding for her. Whether in business or in love, no person of value wants an employee, friend, or lover who is emotionally broke.

Gilda-Gram®
What we believe we deserve is what we receive, nothing more, nothing less.

But there's a hitch. Believing you *deserve* to a payoff is crucial in determining whether you get it or not. YET, just waking up in the morning, rolling out of bed, and *believing* you deserve something because you're alive and breathing falls under the category of undeserving "entitlement," and no one is *entitled* to anything he or she doesn't legitimately earn. How does this work?

Managerial Behavior is one of the college courses I taught to adults returning to college in an accelerated leadership program. To train my students to manage elegantly, one of my requirements was that they complete a team paper. Teams usually comprise five students, and the work needs to be done both inside and outside of class. The course also calls for students to devise grades for one another, with the provision that all team members agree on these grades. To instill a sense of competition in these managers-to-be, I also insisted that no two team members' grades be the same.

Right before the end of the semester, I received an email from Arlene who was furious with Fred who decided he deserved an A for his participation, although he hadn't done a thing. She informed me that it was she who had single-handedly written the majority of the paper. While the others on her team graciously accepted a B, a B+, and a B-, Fred decided to try to overpower the group and assign himself a mightier grade than anyone else. As the group discussed it, they tried to devise a fair solution, but Fred refused to back down.

Fred had lady-killer good looks, and it was obvious he was used to getting his way with most things. To complicate matters, he was also having an affair with one of his teammates, who naturally defended his right to an A. The episode exploded on the last evening of the course. Arlene suddenly blew up, standing in front of the entire class, using mind-blowing expletives to punctuate her anger. She ranted about how hard she had worked on this paper, how she, as a single mom, had to hire a babysitter to meet with the rest of the team on the weekend, and how she has to somehow scrape together the college tuition each semester to pay for school. She volunteered this information as her reason for her taking her college education so seriously.

The rest of the class couldn't believe they were listening to this outburst. Arlene's team leader angrily told her that no one had assigned her the role of overfunctioner for the entire group. He also said he resented the fact that she had gone over his head to complain to me. I calmly asked Fred to explain his side of the story.

Fred began with a belligerent air of entitlement, attempting to sweet-talk his way out of his jam. Only after I continued to press him for the precise details did he finally concede that he really had been negligent in getting his assignment to the rest of the members on time. But he said that he had nonetheless handed in a few paragraphs on the last day, even though the paper had already been completed. Finally, he grumbled that although perhaps he didn't deserve an A after all, he certainly didn't deserve an F. On what basis he concluded that was anyone's guess. But this was the group's decision, and my role was just to act as instigator, motivator, and facilitator.

I turned to the rest of the class to make a teaching opportunity out of this fiasco. I asked how important in life timing is. Fred got the point.

Gilda-Gram®
In life, no one deserves a passing grade just for showing up.

There are no free rides. Everyone must contribute his or her share in order to be rewarded. But although Fred had seemed to get the point, Arlene still had a way to go. She needed to understand that although her personal issues were important to her, they had no bearing on the final paper that was submitted.

When I'm on TV, no one cares about all the sweat that went into our production of the show they're watching. When you attend a concert, no one cares how many times the sound equipment malfunctioned during rehearsal. When you're being interviewed for a job, no one cares about the chaos you experienced that morning when your dog ran out of your house, and you frantically had to scope the neighborhood until you found him. The bottom line is the bottom line, and the only thing that matters is the final result.

On TV, it's what's on the screen. At a concert, it's the sound of the music. At a job interview, it's how well you sell your skills. When a boss requests a report for his boss, either it's submitted as requested, or it's not. There's no grey area. If you contribute effort to meet the goals of a finished product, you deserve a payoff; if you don't, you don't deserve the payoff—no matter how much you want it, how cute you are, or how well you try to convince the planet that you're worth more than what is currently being rewarded to you!

Yes, it's true that plenty of folks out there in the big, bad world get away with reaping benefits they don't deserve, and it irks those of us who do work hard for their just desserts. But there is an overriding law of reciprocity that says, "What you give out, you get back." Consequently,

<u>Gilda-Gram®</u>
Eventually, everything catches up
with those who try to slide by.

On a more obvious level, the same principle presides at the gym: The folks who follow the prescribed regimen are in the best shape. For those innocent bystanders who still become upset to see people getting off without putting in the effort, remember that if you wait long enough, you'll see how it plays out. Believe me, trust me: eventually, everyone *does* get exactly what he or she deserves!!

People who demand payoffs regardless of their deserve-ability, are Wanna-Be's, and they function by forever wanting to be winners, without the requisite sweat. To repeat, there are no free rides. Only through learning that they can't get away with slacking off will they change their approach. And I use every opportunity I can to teach this lesson.

The postscript to the Arlene/Fred debacle is that the rest of the group felt sorry for Fred and awarded him a C for his very meager efforts. Sure, it was not an F, but they each emailed me to say that they had learned a great deal about payoffs and expectations that they would carry into their lives. Most importantly, they learned that they were reluctant to confront.

Confrontation is a big issue for most people, and it takes guts. Each admitted he had fallen short on courage to confront Fred. But I was satisfied that they at least recognized it as an issue for each of them, and if they wanted to succeed as corporate managers and managers of their lives, they would have to master this very important skill.

About a week later, I received an email from Arlene describing an incident that had occurred at her job:

Dear Dr. Gilda,

Monday morning, I was sitting in my director's office when a phone call came in from one of her colleagues. Suddenly, she began to yell and curse, just as I myself had done in class. Then she slammed down the receiver and started to cry. She had replicated the exact same outburst as I had demonstrated in front of my classmates, and I have to admit that it wasn't pretty!

I repeated the words you expressed to me in class: "Don't let your tormentors see you sweat." Moments later, her colleague called me, knowing that I had observed the argument. He said he didn't want to deal with my director because she was "too crazy." I immediately noted how outbursts are read! He was actually laughing about having made her cry. Yes, while my director sat in her office sobbing, her colleague thought her upset was funny.

I said, "You can laugh all you want, but you are not going to speak to me the way you spoke to her. Let's start out on a good note this morning." He laughed some more, and said, "Arlene, you are something else!'" At that moment, I knew that I had finally mastered my emotions and that from then on, I would set up appropriate boundaries that demanded respect.

Thank you so much, Dr. Gilda, for teaching me

this very valuable lesson.
Love,
Arlene

From the experience she had in class, Arlene had obviously learned some difficult lessons: to communicate deliberately yet calmly, to construct personal boundaries, and to ask for what she wanted in a way she would be heard. Actually, in this case, she *told* her director's colleague that she was not going to accept his poor treatment. Although he laughed and praised her professionalism, he learned that Arlene demanded his respect. And Arlene learned that she would attract more flies with honey than she would with vinegar!

I was so proud of this woman. And I felt quite accomplished. Life defines us by how we navigate the obstacles in our path. For sure, if you're on this planet, you'll certainly experience plenty of obstacles. But you'll have plenty of company. And plenty of opportunity to correct other people's treatment of you!

Many people mistakenly believe that life is neatly separated into personal and professional compartments. They think that they can be strong in one area even while the other one is crumbling. In truth, segmented lives don't exist. Observe any person going through a divorce and see how unfocused and disconnected they also are at work. We enact the image we have of ourselves in everything we do, whether at work or at play. Our behavior towards others is a natural extension of how we feel about ourselves. Further, how we feel about ourselves determines the types of people we attract. This concept explains the old adage as to why the rich get richer and the poor stay poor. The reasoning is simple:

<u>Gilda-Gram®</u>
People attract people like themselves.

Personal Full Disclosure: I was once a Wanna Be Loser. I stayed in jobs with abusive bosses and remained in some disrespectful relationships for much too long. People stay stuck in dead-end jobs and relationships because they're afraid they can't do better. They rationalize staying because they don't want to upset their children, or lower their income.

These are our convenient excuses, our crutches, each of us holding a different one dear. We unload our sorrows onto friends who think they're doing us well by lending an ear. But if anything, by just dumping our discontent and resentment into a conversation without actually doing something to change it, we continue our misery.

In my case, since I was spoon-fed the fairy tales during my youngest years, I fantasized that someone, anyone, would rescue me from my mates and jobs, like waiting to be "discovered" or "rescued" by a prince. But no one came. Actually, no one can. (That's why I wrote

11

my book, "Don't Bet on the Prince!")   In the end, no one can save us from ourselves but we, ourselves.

For me, as "luck" would have it (And I believe now that we make our own "luck"!), the stress of my unhappiness caused crippling back pain that landed me in a thick, uncomfortable back brace. The pain was dreadful, but now, looking back, it turned out to be a blessing in disguise, because it became imperative for me to alter the way I was living. Who woulda thunk? But also, who wants to alter her entire life? Because of that experience, I created this:

<u>Gilda-Gram®</u>
**When something happens *to* us,
it really happens *for* us.**

The big challenge is for each of us to uncover what we're supposed to learn from every situation. And that's not easy while we're undergoing our pain!! Since I'm the Country Music Doctor (See **www.CountryCures.org**), I always seek support for my teachings from the tunes and lyrics of Country Music. On their "Gravity" album, Country Music artists, Big & Rich have a poignant and insightful single called, "Thank God for Pain." Yes! Despite the fact that we hate it, pain pushes us to open our eyes, and FINALLY reassess things that are draining us. It's sure not easy. But once we derive it, the payoff is tremendous!

When I examined my own discontent, I knew I needed to let go of the so-called "secure" things that weren't so secure after all. These things were making me ill. I didn't know what my future held—and that was so scary for such a take-charge personality—but as soon as I changed my status quo, something amazing occurred. In place of the security I *thought* I had, I discovered newfound freedom, independence, and a belief that I *deserved* to be at peace and happy. Wow!

I expanded the management consulting work I had casually begun in corporate America, and I found that I loved making a difference in the lives of large audiences of people, as well as in their bottom lines. I was awarded the honored title of "Best Speaker in America" by a professional magazine. I conducted corporate seminars, and I became a college professor. My motivational speaking led to TV shows, book deals, movies, interviews, and international recognition. What a change for someone who was once scared and stuck in Wanna-Be mentality!

Initially, of course, I was terrified of making any sort of drastic life change! Anybody would be, because new territory is supposed to frighten us. But I also knew that my life was not acceptable as it had become. And, in fact, it was physically damaging me.

This experience showed me courage buried inside me that I didn't even know I had. I became a better, more compassionate relationship expert, and champion for self-growth. Certainly, if I could take such leaps, so can you!

Even today, I sometimes stumble with fear that paralyzes me. That's when I go inside, do a lot of self-talk, and remember my lessons about where I still want to go, and the blockages that fear causes. Nobody breathing can avoid occasional stumbling blocks. We're *all* works in progress! And that's a good thing, because it reminds us we're alive.

CHAPTER 2

WHERE ARE YOU NOW?

No matter where you are living, with whom you are involved, or how much or how little money you possess,

Gilda-Gram®
Your life evolves from your regard for yourself.

Your regard for yourself is what we call "self-esteem." I prefer to call it "self-worth," because we are all worthy of so much more than we acknowledge. People with low self-worth often try to feel better about themselves by impressing others with material flash, or trying to overpower them with manipulative put-downs. Many guys at some alleged millionaire dating sites try to impress women with their "toys" of yachts, cars, travel photos, homes, and more. When they come across a woman who wants to know *them*, rather than their toys, they are flummoxed. Where would they go without their "masks" of achievement?

Or, take some of the women who are similarly

15

trying to nail one of these millionaires. How do they present themselves? They show a lot of skin, and display their fine body, or post photos from ten or twenty years ago. They are all trying to mask a feeling of little worth. Without their cover-ups, they'd crumble.

How do you know if your own self-worth is healthy? For one thing, examine the externals in your life: the car you drive, the clothes you wear, the jewelry you adorn, the house you live in, the neighborhood you enjoy, the company you keep. Do you have them for their functionality, or are they serving the purpose of status? If you require a car for transportation, do you need to drive one that's top of the line? When you adorn your body, do your garments have to be designer duds? When you post your photo on social media, are you interested in deception or reality? These are questions only you can answer within yourself.

We live in a culture laden with labels. But a shirt is a shirt is a shirt. How taken in are you with status seeking? When my friend's daughter was merely three, she told me that her mom had just bought her jeans. I asked, "What kind of jeans?" (meaning, what was their color and style?). But this little tyke responded, "They're *designer* jeans, of course!" If a three-year-old is indoctrinated this way, imagine how much more saturated with status symbols she will yet become when she's an adult.

While I was teaching a psychology course, mid-sentence, I casually glanced out the classroom's window. Since the room was on the second floor overlooking a private alley, I couldn't help but notice a gorgeous, shiny, antique Rolls Royce in mint condition. The automobile was so extraordinary looking, I halted what I was saying and just stared. Here I was, discussing self-worth, and right in front of me was this obvious extension of someone's ego.

I instructed my students to leave their seats and take a look. As they ohhh-ed and ahhh-ed, I said, "That is an example of someone who needs to trumpet his self-worth, which is undoubtedly not as high as he'd like it to be." (I [perhaps unjustly] just assumed the owner was a *he*.) The class rushed to the window to observe the spectacle, and we all had a good laugh before returning to the topic at hand.

Exactly one week later, a girlfriend and I met up with her new boyfriend at the restaurant he owned. Sitting with him was a very attractive man who I was immediately drawn to. He and I spoke for hours, and I especially enjoyed his lively sense of humor. He asked me out for the following weekend and I accepted.

During the week, we spoke on the phone several times, and we got along well. When he came to pick me up, there he was, driving the same antique Rolls I had spotted outside the classroom window while I was teaching. Yes, it was his car that had been parked in that alleyway. Shocked by the coincidence, I told him the story, and we chuckled. But the car was a tip-off of who this guy really *wasn't*.

Because I enjoyed laughing with him, I chose to ignore the obvious signs that followed, like the way he tailed after my girlfriend's wealthy boyfriend, like the famous names he continued to drop as being his "dear" friends, like the constant need he had to get attention wherever he went. After three casual dates, I decided that, as attractive as he was, this guy was too insecure for me. I could have saved us both a lot of time had I only followed my own lessons from the start.

Oftentimes, the material things a person sports are cover-ups for an emotional void too painful to confront. These ostentatious people may *need* to achieve self-worth so badly that they may even go into debt to don attention-getters that others will admire.

A friend of mine was a maître d' at an expensive catering hall. He discovered that it was not unusual for him to have to drive home the parents of a bride after they had just spent a whopping five or six figures throwing their splashy wedding. He found that they either lacked a car, or they just couldn't afford to take a cab home from the wedding they had thrown for the sole purpose of impressing others!

Status seekers say they *want* these goodies, but in actuality, they *need* them for a personal ego boost. Veronica projected her *want*, while Betty projected her *need*. Marilyn also projected her need. Each woman sought a soul mate, but each went about it in a different way. The most successful among them, Veronica, knew that feeling good must always begin with her.

Gilda-Gram®
**Before you seek a soul mate, or a soul job,
unearth your own soul.**

Consider these 3 sequential steps to soul seeking before you get out of bed each day:

1. Discover what you need.
2. Determine what you want.
3. Project what you believe you *deserve to get.*

Needs and wants are very different. Needs are what you *must have to survive* (and they do not include a Rolls Royce!) Wants are what you *prefer to have to feel good.* When you are hungry your body alerts you that you *need* to eat. But what kind of food will you choose? Your choice of food is your want. What if you salivate at the thought of a steak, yet that is not available? Temporarily, to allay your hunger, a bag of nuts could suffice. So although your desired want would not be met, your bodily need to eat would nonetheless be satisfied.

In 1943, psychologist Abraham Maslow wrote a paper called "A Theory of Human Motivation" in which he formulated a hierarchy of human needs. This hierarchy has become the foundation for understanding what drives people's actions. On the very lowest level, the hierarchy shows how we *need* to be fed, to be clothed, and to be protected from bodily harm. These are our Physiological and Security needs, and they are followed by less vital needs on a hierarchy of importance.

Maslow's ladder, starting at the bottom with Number 1, from lower to higher level needs is:

5) Self-Actualization (being all you can be)
4) Esteem
3) Love
2) Safety
1) Physiological

As the lower needs are met, people naturally progress to higher ones. But until each level is at least somewhat satisfied, people won't seek gratification on the next higher rung. Maslow also indicated that people will travel up and down the Needs Hierarchy, depending on where they are in their lives.

Everyone functions at a particular Needs Level. On what Level are YOU functioning now?

Discovering Your Needs Level

Number each of the following statements in their order of importance to you, making the most important #1, and the least important #5.

___1. When I'm hungry, I stop what I'm doing to eat. (Physiological)

___2. A steady and secure job is most important to me. (Safety)

___3 My main goal is to be happy. (Self-Actualization)

___4. I feel confident promoting myself. (Esteem)

___5. I am always available for someone I care for. (Love)

Self-Discovery

Which of these needs did you find to be most important in your life right now?

The questions on this and all the quizzes that follow are meant to get you to think about issues you have not considered before. There are no right or wrong answers, but your responses will guide you on your path to becoming a Will-Be Winner.

Carmella was dating Cliff for a year. During their time together, Cliff often did not demonstrate the kind of affection Carmella expected. She acknowledged that his divorce was ongoing and difficult, but she assumed their passion was powerful enough to make him forget his pain. I explained to Carmella that no matter what she did, Cliff was currently functioning at his two lowest Needs Levels, Physiological, which defined how he would fend for himself without his wife and children, and Safety, which explained where he would securely live.

These two Needs are basic to survival, and Cliff could only muster up enough energy for them during these excruciating times. Sure, his relationship with Carmella was pleasant, and the sex was invigorating, but to Carmella's disappointment, Cliff's major concerns were issues other than her. What emotionally healthy woman would accept this kind of treatment?

Gilda-Gram®
A person in the <u>ING</u> position--divorc<u>ING</u>, separat<u>ING</u>, griev<u>ING</u>—is functioning at the two lowest Needs Levels: Physiological and Safety. This person is struggling for survival, and is unable to rise to the third Needs Level of Love.

At this time, Cliff was definitely not ready to give Carmella what she said she *needed*. But my discussion with Carmella got her to question why she would want a man who was in the ING position when she said that she herself *needed* more. And this is precisely my point. Many people think they *need* something when they really only *want* it.

Gilda-Gram®
If you don't know what you need, you won't get what you want.

I explained to Carmella that if she really *needed*

intimacy leading to marriage, she would not have chosen Cliff. After completing the quiz, she finally began to wonder why she was pursuing someone who was not emotionally available. She considered Item #3, Love, to be her most important need, but she also had to admit that Cliff was obviously stuck on #1 and #2.

With her new insight, although she felt awful about it, she pushed herself to begin dating more available partners. At last, she came to grips with the fact that she didn't *need* any relationship to survive. But she agreed that whatever relationship she would find would have to lead to permanence.

It was painful for her to admit that she had been languishing in a love affair that she enjoyed, but which merely fulfilled her *wants*. Yet, once she saw the light, she was able to change her course, and find someone more available. Today, she's happily married to a husband who is capable of *adoring* her.

Along the same lines, Kristi met Marc after he had been divorced for three years. After that amount of time, she surmised that he had finished his grievING and would now be ready to settle down. They fell in love and dated for six months before they decided to live together.

Once under the same roof, Kristi discovered that although Marc was finished grievING for his ex-wife, he was still grievING over the business he had foolishly left when his marriage was folding. He had been a partner in a very lucrative law firm, and without thinking, he sold out to his other partners during his emotionally painful breakup. Now that his marriage was over and he had moved on, he looked back and regretted how thoughtless he had been to walk out on such a thriving career.

It was early September and Kristi had to conduct a business trip near Niagara Falls, to which she needed to fly. Since she had a few free days between her scheduled meetings, and since the setting is such a romantic spot for love, Cliff decided to make the eight-hour drive to join her there. The idea of the two of them renewing their commitment alongside the gushing waters absolutely thrilled Kristi.

On the second day of their extraordinary time together, as they strolled by the falls, Marc's cell phone suddenly rang. It was a call from the chief counsel of the law firm Marc had left. The guy said he wanted to meet with Marc. Marc didn't ask about the nature of the meeting, didn't suggest they do it when he returned from vacation, and certainly did not consider Kristi's feelings. Instead, he quickly jumped in his car and drove the eight hours home without stopping. All he could think of was regaining his previous position and business status. A shocked Kristi just stood there and cried. After she completed her own business, she continued to cry on her plane trip home.

Luckily, she came upon this quiz, Discovering Your Needs Level. When she took it, she found that, like Carmella, she was positioned on Level #3, Love. However, the quiz pushed her to admit that Marc was on Level #4, Esteem. Like a lot of people who use their job to pump their ego, Marc desperately sought to feel better about himself by regaining what he once had, but threw away. Unfortunately, he did not know that

Gilda-Gram®
Once it's over, you can never return to the past in the same way.

As it turned out, the chief counsel didn't want to re-hire Marc at all; he just wanted to pick his brain for valuable information from which he and the firm could benefit. Marc left the meeting feeling dejected.

Within weeks, an emotionally more confident Kristi left Marc because she was feeling unfulfilled in their union. She had finally gotten it: while he was still searching to fill his Esteem need, Marc could not be focusing on their Love.

For as long as I've been dispensing relationship advice, this is one of the most difficult concepts for clients to hear: Anyone in *any kind* of ING position will remain in the ING position until he or she is ready to leave it. No matter how gorgeous, rich, thin, educated, confident, or anything else you are, you will never, never, never, *do you hear me??* NEVER be able to push someone onto another Needs Level. This concept applies to both the personal and professional realm. If someone is to move from one Level to another, they must do it alone.

I counsel people with issues in both the bedroom and the boardroom. When it comes to the boardroom, one of the most often asked questions I get is how to ask the boss for a raise.

My client, Grace, was flabbergasted when an interviewee for a job came to see her, bills in hand. As soon as they began the interview, he neatly laid out each and every one of them so that Grace could see how badly he *needed* the job. She apologized to this poor soul, and said that the position was based solely on the value a candidate could bring to the company, not on his monetary need. Unfortunately, this job candidate had not differentiated between his needs and wants, and misconstrued that this interviewer would feel sorry enough for him to reward him for his impoverishment. If anything, his supposition backfired when Grace was turned off by this antic. Companies are not welfare agencies, and life is not a charity event.

Recognize where you and others are positioned on the Needs Hierarchy. Then, differentiate between your own needs and wants. Having this skill will offer you protection against wasting time and getting hurt. Whether it's in business or in your personal life,

Gilda-Gram®
Protect yourself from a *want* you may crave, while dismissing a *need* you must have.

So that you don't end up like Grace's job candidate, ask for what you believe you deserve, based on what you earned, and what you have to offer.

As you begin to analyze your own situation, you will see that your needs are limited, but your wants can be great. No one *needs* to win the lottery, but lots of people *want* to. A person starved for affection may find herself aimlessly sleeping with multiple partners to fill her emotional void. She may tell herself she *needs* sex, but in actuality, she *wants* to be wanted. *Want* can be so strong that it can mimic *need*. So the distinction between the two must be defined well before you pursue any goal.

Also differentiate between *need* and *neediness*. Contrary to popular misconception, it's not only women who are needy. While needs are necessities people require to sustain themselves, neediness is pure dependency. Relying on a partner or a job for your total salvation can be tricky. If your partner leaves or your job dries up, if you don't have a strong backbone, you'll be left to fend for yourself with no backup. And if you mistakenly believe you'll replace one job or partner with another, if you're as needy as Marilyn, you will probably turn off the very people you will long to attract.

Carmella learned that she could survive without being in a close relationship. Because she had been in the *wrong* relationship, she ended up becoming totally drained. Luckily, she realized that her *want* to be involved with Cliff had to change into a *need* to remove herself from the pain.

The best way to guarantee a good life is to provide yourself with a strong dose of independence. Of course, you'll probably still need a job to earn a living, and you'll still want a partner to share your life. But when you're independent, rather than needy, you won't be in such a hurry to choose, and consequently make the wrong decision in your haste.

The concept of differentiating between *need* and *want* applies to all aspects of life, whether it's loving someone or even negotiating to buy a house. *Wanting*, rather than *needing*, sends the message that if someone or something is not available, you will live just fine. Paradoxically, with that attitude, the less emotionally desperate you seem, the more your potential provider will value your participation. This is just one of life's ironies, but it's the reason why the people we like the least are interested in us, and the job we least want is the one that is put on the table.

So now you know why desperate singles don't connect, and desperate job seekers don't land the job of their dreams. Yet, as ironic as all this seems, it provides an important life lesson:

Gilda-Gram®
**Know what you want, and know what you need.
But never be too desperate for either.**

As I told Arlene, "Never let your tormentor see you sweat." Without *your* desperation, people will be more able to evaluate *their* desire to meet your goals. Much of what they decide to ultimately offer has to do with what you project you *deserve*. Would you fall prey to someone who says he *needs* a job, or would you be more impressed when he offers reasons for *why he deserves it?*

Everyone has a Deserve Level. Deserve is not synonymous with entitlement. The way you project that you Deserve something will determine whether your request is judged as worthy.

Gilda-Gram®
**Project your Deserve Level
in language of *want,* not *need.***

With a listener who is primed to give you what you want, you'll have to be equipped to ask for it in a manner he can hear. Elegant asking consists of a 5-step process. Find out what this process is in the next chapter, Chapter 3

CHAPTER 3

THE 5 STEPS TO ASKING

Asking for what you believe you deserve involves 5 simple steps:

1) Set your goal.
2) Assess its availability.
3) Determine whether you *want* it or *need* it.
4) Be a giver before a getter.
5) Project why you deserve to get your goal.

Step #1: Setting Your Goal

Before you go about blurting out what you "really, really want," as the song goes, be sure your goal is a S.M.A.R.T. one. It must be:

S: Specific
M: Measurable
A: Achievable
R: Real
T: Time-Sensitive

A *specific* goal directs vague wishes such as "I

want a new job" or "I want to improve my marriage" into specific details like, "I want a new *writing* job" or "I want to learn how to deal with my husband's ex." Once you know exactly where you're going, be sure you are aware of its *measurability* so you can determine if you've gotten there. Also be certain that the goal is *achievable* so that you are not wasting your effort.

In other words, there are other factors to take into consideration, like other people's willingness to help you. Further, be sure your goal is *real* rather than just a long held fantasy that makes you smile. Finally, have a timeline for achieving your goal. If your goal is not *time-sensitive*, you may work forever to get it, not recognizing when to halt your efforts. Making sure your goal is S.M.A.R.T. prepares you for goal achievement.

Step #2: Assessing Your Goal's Availability

If your goal involves another person, is that person anxious to be part of your mission, or is he apathetic? Marian was having second thoughts about marrying her fiancé. She suggested they see a relationship therapist before they tied the knot. But Mel was adamantly opposed to getting any kind of help. He said he loved Marian, and he wondered why that was just not enough for her. He ignored her pleas when she said she wasn't happy.

Do you have a goal that's dependent on the cooperation of someone else? If that person is unwilling to comply with your wish, what are you willing to make your next step?

Step #3: Determining Whether You Want Your Goal or Need Your Goal

For Marian, because she was suffering personal pain, she decided that she *needed* to feel better about the relationship before she committed herself to marriage. Since Mel refused to join her, she chose to seek counseling on her own. Had it been just a want, she might have postponed the help, married Mel, and found out later that the union was a mistake.

Marian chose to seek counseling on her own. She received the help she needed and she also sent a silent message to Mel that even if he were unwilling to take her concerns seriously, she would take care of herself.

As it turned out, therapy taught her that she was having fears of commitment based on the fact that her parents divorced when she was a little girl. She worked through her anguish and she and Mel have been happily wed for five years. If she hadn't taken the reins herself, she might have unconsciously sabotaged the marriage later.

Step #4: Giving, Just Because It Feels Good

Years ago, when my name was beginning to become well known, I attended a business networking party. People from different Fortune 500 companies were mulling about, cocktail glass in one hand, business card in another, trying to impress each other, hoping to make contacts that would pay off. The overall scene was more "Tell me what you can do for me," rather than "Let me share what I can do for you."

Amid the clatter of chatter, an unfamiliar woman approached me and said, "I know you're Dr. Gilda and that you make speeches and do seminars in corporations. My name is Mary Ellen Smith and I sell corporate art work. The next time you're at one of your clients, could you please just leave them my card?" I stood there, dumbfounded and thought, "Why should I do this for this woman I don't even know? Besides, if I'm in the midst of selling my own program, why would I choose to divert a potential customer's attention to something so totally different?"

This Mary Ellen never even tried to sell me on why she deserved my efforts. She just whipped out her card and thrust it into my hand. Gracefully, I excused myself and dropped her card into the nearest trashcan I saw. A few seconds later, disappointed with the attitude of this "gimme" crowd, I was out the door and in my car heading home.

The "gimme" attitude not only doesn't get anyone anywhere, it also turns off a listener who may potentially be able to help you. If you suffer from them, get rid of your "gimmes," and replace them with *secure relationships you nurture*. That's what was missing in the demand that opportunistic Mary Ellen made of me. Share knowledge, networks, and compassion, not to gain anything back, but to spread your wealth of knowledge and connections with someone who can use it—and who *deserves* it!

Giving is the nicest thing we can do for someone. And if you're wondering what's in it for you?, the Law of Reciprocity guarantees that what we give out, we get back. Often, this "get back" is not even from the person to whom you gave. However, understanding this Law will calm those people concerned about being "used." Just protect your precious boundaries, and give from the surplus you have, not from what you require to survive.

Yes, goodness comes back somehow, somewhere, from someone, and perhaps not from the person to whom you originally gave. It's mystical! I wish more people knew this.

Earlier, I named two signs of a person's low self-esteem: materialism and manipulation. The next emailer is the epitome of attempted manipulation in an effort to make himself shine. Can you detect how?

Dear Dr. Gilda,

I am a tax attorney, and last year, I remember thinking that it was the summer of my deceased mother-in-law. I had taken on the thankless job of working on her estate until it was settled that summer. The problems were ongoing, and I forever had to remain on top of everything for which I was not being paid. I reasoned that I was doing this for my wife of ten years.

After the paperwork was completed, although my wife did say thank you, it seemed that she accepted all I did as a matter of course, similar to my taking out the garbage. This summer, a similar thing happened. This time it became the summer of my stepdaughter, a college student. She did not do so well in one of her courses, and I took it upon myself to tutor her so she could have a second chance at a final exam. In return for my kindness, yes, she did thank me, but she also criticized my tutoring more than once, and often put her boyfriend before her schoolwork and studying.

My wife and I have had a rocky relationship since we were married. During a recent heated argument, I lost my temper and screamed that I would not celebrate her birthday, and I would also not take her on our usual summer vacation. So now my wife has spitefully decided to go on vacation with her daughter, leaving me in the lurch.
Robert

Dear Robert,
Is there a question somewhere embedded in your marital complaint? It appears that you want to be paid, thanked and loved to compensate for your rocky marriage. This is called "conditional giving," and it goes against everything I stand for, teach, and write. If things you did for this family in the past had gone unappreciated, why do you continue doing more?

Did you undertake your actions so you could keep reminding them of your supposed benevolence?

You say you were thanked by both your wife and her daughter, but you didn't like the way they thanked you. That seems awfully controlling.

What exactly did you want them to do? In essence, no matter how anyone thanks you, it will never compensate for the fact that your marriage is in trouble and it needs either to be repaired or discarded. You say this discord has continued for 10 miserable years. Why would you prefer to browbeat this family instead of taking a stand to either stay, and make the relationship better, or leave in a dignified manner?

To be blunt, you stay there as a tormentor because your own self esteem is shaky and you need to overpower others to feel better about yourself. Undoubtedly, your wife has shaky self-esteem, too, because she has also been willing to put up with this dance you're both doing.

Appreciation must be earned through respectful communication devoid of screams and threats. Your nasty words are bullying tactics that cannot be withdrawn after they're issued. Obviously, you raged at your wife one too many times, and she finally called your bluff. Actually, this may be a sign that she's about to take a stand regarding the way things have been. I'm proud of her for taking care of herself, and providing the vacation that you threatened to withhold. Who do you think you are to punish an adult that way? No healthy grownup would allow herself to be tormented that way. At least one party in your marriage is becoming healthier.

When you learn the nature of unconditional giving you'll find how much more you can get in return, without having to growl, scowl, or intimidate. You're apparently well versed in tax law. Now it's time to do some graduate work in the law of reciprocity.
Dr. Gilda

Compare Robert's conditional giving with that of Lois who owns a new age shop filled with spiritual books, tapes, CD's, silver jewelry, angels, and candles. During a big blackout, instead of taking advantage of the people as some other storeowners did, Lois kept her shop open until 2:15 AM and sold her candles at half price. She said she didn't want to price-gauge anyone when they were in such dire need of illumination. As a result of her generosity, she ended up selling out all her merchandise. Not only had she done a service to her community, but her kind heart unwittingly also attracted lots of new customers who continued to return. That's the way the Law of Reciprocity works.

People like Robert need huge doses of applause to compensate for their neediness for love. People like Lois can live without this sort of flash because their self-esteem is secure.

Step #5: Communicating WHY You Deserve to Get

My email back to Robert says it all. He had been less than gracious with his wife when he enumerated each and every thing he had done for her, and how he wanted his thanks delivered. As it turned out, he discovered that he wasn't the only one who could enumerate. Finally, after 10 years of suffering, his wife had the gumption to enumerate herself as Number 1! Good for her.

Asking for something is a difficult task for most people. The Roberts of the world find it more comfortable to intimate than request. He couldn't even ask me for the help he took the time to seek in his e-mail. Sales training programs make it a point to specifically teach their sales force to *ask* for the order. Of course, no one wants to set herself up to be turned down. But the alternative to asking is *not* asking. And if you don't ask, you are then left to wonder what would have been if only you had followed your desire. If you're in a restaurant, and you don't ask for the seat by the window, you will continue to get the one by the kitchen.

People who are especially afflicted by the inability to articulate their desires are fearful that their respondents may reject them or even abandon them. They also fear that they will appear too aggressive, or, worse, that they won't be liked. However, unless they ask for what they want, they project that they don't believe they *deserve* to get anything more than what they already have.

CHAPTER 4

THE POWER OF DESERVE

I first discovered the power of Deserve Level while training salespeople at a seminar. On an index card, I asked them to write the earnings they believed they deserved in the upcoming year. We sealed the cards into envelopes, I collected them, and when the year was up, we re-convened. Most of the group had forgotten they had even performed this task. But after I re-distributed the cards, there were "ohhh's" and "ahhh's" from an audience amazed that, with few exceptions, each person had earned what he believed he would, within a few thousand dollars of what he or she had written!

I continue to incorporate this exercise into my work worldwide, whether the topic is business or romance. The results are always the same. For sure, we create for ourselves exactly what we believe we deserve to get.

Deserve Level is the electrical wiring that delineates our boundaries and commands respect. It lets people know where *we* stand, so they can decide where *they* stand regarding us. When we send messages that we have earned the right to be deserving, people unconsciously treat us as we are "telling" them to. What is YOUR Deserve Level? Let's find out.

Your Deserve Level

List every activity you spend more than 10 minutes doing over the course of one day. Beside each item, note whether the activity is for you, your family, your job, your mate, or others.

Self-Discovery

1. What do you spend the most time doing?
2. Is this how you *need* to spend your time or how you *want* to spend your time?
3. How do you believe you *deserve* to spend your time?

This quiz analyzes your time management. Time management is a subtle autobiography that tells more about you than you realize.

Gilda-Gram®
The way you spend your time
reflects how you value yourself.

Mary discovered that she spent the majority of her time doing chores for her children and spouse. Time was abundant for everyone else's *needs* but there was never any time left for the *wants* that she enjoyed. By voiding her own interests from her day, she was inadvertently sending the message that she was meaningless, and that she deserved little respect. No wonder her husband and family took her for granted. If we respect our own use of time, we are defined not as somebody's spouse, parent, daughter, father, employee, or slave, but as *somebody!*

<u>Gilda-Gram®</u>
Somebodies communicate *that* they deserve and *what* they deserve.

Each emotionally abused and physically battered woman I've worked with has a deficit in Deserve Level. Each of these women learned somewhere in her life that she *deserved* no more than the poor treatment she was getting.

I sat with one woman on a TV talk show who was learning for the first time that her husband had cheated with many of their neighbors. After this woman heard the news and cried, she was quick to rationalize, "All men cheat." Because of her belief about "all men," she clearly attracted a cheater as a mate. Although she was upset about her discovery, she conceded that this is the way love is. As much as Terry tried to dismiss this fact, she had to recognize that she was manifesting into her life what she really believed she deserved—which was not very much.

The way to break negative habits is to substitute more positive designs. Terry began to discriminate between her *needs* and *wants*. She started to learn that by considering her own requirements as least important, everyone followed her lead. As strange as this sounds, we are totally in control of the way others treat us. Whenever someone approaches us, either calmly or gruffly, the way we respond positions him or her to either continue behaving as they are or to alter their ways.

Gilda-Gram®
What we accept, we teach.

Dear Dr. Gilda:

I'm a 30-year-old liberated lady who has been on the pill for the two years I've been with my boyfriend. It's getting expensive, and I think he should share the cost. The problem is that I don't know him well enough to discuss money with him.
Carrie

Dear Carrie:

At first, this struck me as a peculiar question. You're intimate with this guy, and intimate partners ought to be able to discuss anything, especially since you've been involved for two long years. But your question really reveals a lot about you, and the way you're dealing in this affair.

What are your needs? What are your wants? Do you need him to help defray the cost of your birth control, or do you really want him to demonstrate more consideration for you in every aspect of your life together? The fact that you think you are liberated must also be re-thought because "liberated ladies" are able to communicate what's on their mind without fear of reprisals. Are you afraid you'll discover how he truly values you? Are you afraid that this may be a deal breaker that will ultimately mean the end of the romance?

Since no birth control method is 100 percent safe, what would happen if you had an accidental pregnancy? Or, if you contracted an STD? Are you afraid that his response to your request for help would tell you that his real feelings for you are not as strong as you'd like?

If you fear making a fateful faux pas that would lose this man, you are accepting, and thereby teaching him that you're a pushover regarding your desires. If that is the case, your fears will continue to hold you back from expressing yourself in other, even more important, ways.

Before any intimate relationship can continue, you should: 1) consider your real goal in asking for financial help, 2) assess its possibility, for example, determining whether he actually has the money, 3) determine whether you want it or need it, 4) work insightfully to achieve it, possibly by practicing your request, and 5) communicate why you deserve it. While I call these my 5 Steps to Asking, they are also the basis for a healthy relationship that is slated to survive.

Carrie, you've been involved with this guy not for two days or two months, but for two years! What other burning issues have you neglected to discuss with him? Your answers to these questions will reveal much about your future together.
Dr. Gilda

Clearly, Carrie didn't believe she deserved to ask for what she wanted. There's no doubt that asking for something is tough, especially if you're not used to doing it. Now that you have learned the 5 Steps for Asking, in the next quiz you will get to practice this graceful art. Yes, this is an art form, and an art form requires practice. Take the quiz and learn whether you have to sharpen your technique.

How to Ask

Think of one person in your past you neglected to ask for something. What did you miss out on? Practice the 5 Steps for Asking. To allay your discomfort, keep remembering that if you don't ask, you won't get!

Self-Discovery

1. How did you feel about asking?

2. Did you achieve the response you intended?

If you discovered that you are not comfortable expressing yourself clearly, consider that you are not willing to communicate honestly. If that is the case, your feelings are still your feelings, and they will not just disappear, but will remain buried inside you, which is not healthy. Eventually, these feelings will show themselves through seemingly unrelated behavior, like a short temperedness with the one you love, or an over-indulgence in food, liquor, or other substances to camouflage your real feelings.

The only cure for your reluctance to ask is to feel confident, communicate your honest intentions, and remind yourself that you won't allow yourself to be a pushover. When you do that, you'll truly become an It Person! The next chapter, Chapter 5, will show you how.

CHAPTER 5

BE AN "IT" PERSON

From the quiz above, did you find that you felt really uncomfortable asking for something you believed you deserved? Well, get this: You DO deserve to attract good things into your life! So now the question is: Do you open yourself up to receive them?

In order to receive good things, you must set yourself up as Number 1 the same way Robert's wife did. Do you have the guts to treat yourself that well? This is a difficult concept for many people, but especially for those who fear that if they honor themselves above others, they will be called "selfish." In our culture, "selfish" is not a kind word.

Are you one of those folks concerned about what others call you? If you are, define "selfish" differently. It does not mean dismissing others' needs; rather, it stands for healthy "self regard."

Think of being selfish as the act of putting yourself first in support of YOU. If you don't support your needs, who will? You know that when you *need* to eat, you do. When you *need* to find shelter, you will. Similarly, when you *need* to honor yourself, you absolutely, positively MUST.

Of course, regarding yourself too greatly, and at the expense of those around you, is an obstacle to a healthy relationship. In life, the success of our actions, as well as their consequences, are all measured in terms of degree. If you're a person who always talks about, considers, and supports the "me, me, me" notion to the exclusion of everyone around you, that is a problem.

Eleanor was going out with a politician who would spend his days emailing her the articles that were written about him in every newspaper. He never asked about or tried to get to know her. He was self-serving in the truest sense of the word. Eventually, Eleanor tired of this one-sided relationship and this guy who she had nicknamed "Me, Me, Me."

On the other hand, if you never share, consider, or support your beliefs and desires, that sets you up to be nothing more than a dishrag. And that behavior is "self*less*" or, being without a self. John was the typical Mr. Nice Guy who always ended up being taken advantage of. It's one thing to be nice, but it's another thing to give away your soul. Finally, after he was passed over for one promotion after another, he got the point. It was time for him to value himself, so others would, in turn, value him.

John began by learning to say "no" to requests

that would give away too much of him. At first, it was difficult for this kind man to deny people's requests. But when he realized that he never had enough energy or time left for himself, he knew things had to change. When his neighbor asked to borrow the car that he planned to take on a fishing trip, for the first time, he replied that he couldn't loan it to him. At last, he learned to:

Gilda-Gram®
Give from the overflow, not from the core.

John kept this Gilda-Gram® in his shirt pocket to remind him to retain his core energy for himself. Then, whatever surplus he had left, he could give away to others. In this manner, instead of being selfless, he became self-caring. Immediately, he noticed the difference in how he felt!

One day, while I was shopping at a mall, I noticed a beautiful five-year-old girl. I said to her, "You are so pretty." Innocently, she responded, "I know." Her mother jumped in to scold her for "sounding conceited." The message to the child was to play down her shining star. The little girl looked perplexed. I winked and said, "If you just say, 'Thank you,' everyone will know that you know you're special."

As an adult, do you believe you're special? Or do you think your self-worth has room for improvement?

Dear Dr. Gilda:

My boyfriend just dumped me and I am devastated. We were together for 7 years, and I know that he had been cheating on me throughout our romance, but I chose to look the other way.

Now he has decided to move in with one of the trashy women he had been seeing behind my back. She's disgusting, she's loud, and she has two nasty kids. I don't know what he sees in her, and I can't stop thinking of the two of them together.

By the way, I have always had low self-esteem. My mother was an alcoholic and always put me down. I left home as soon as I was able to support myself. I always end up with men who are bad for me, but they offer some financial support, so I won't feel as helpless as I did when I was growing up. Now that my boyfriend has left, I feel even worse about myself than ever. Please help me!
Margaret

Dear Margaret,

You mention your low self-esteem, as though it is an unimportant detail. In fact, that is the reason you attracted this loser to begin with, the reason you chose to ignore his cheating all these years, and the reason you stayed, despite feeling horrible. Anyone with low self-esteem won't attract and be able to sustain a healthy relationship.

For those seven long years, you communicated dishonestly by not confronting your boyfriend. Your goal was to be liked, instead of respected. So you unconsciously set yourself up to be emotionally abused.

People with low self-esteem attract other people with low self-esteem. So if you didn't mind being an emotional punching bag, your guy probably delighted in doing the emotional punching. While he was supporting your poor image of yourself, he was making himself feel mighty by disrespecting you. Since this disrespect reminded you of how your own mother treated you, it was familiar territory, and so it felt okay.

Sadly, the more you accepted your boyfriend's "less-than" treatment, the more you taught him that his behavior could continue. These are the kinds of situations low self-esteem attracts.

Time will cure your broken heart, but you will not attract a man who is emotionally healthy until you become emotionally healthy yourself. Allow yourself this time alone for mourning and healing. Now spend your energy improving your feelings of self-worth. My book, "I'm Worth Loving! Here's Why." will help you. Dr. Gilda

Like many other people, Margaret repeatedly used her sorry childhood as her easy excuse for her low self-esteem. To compensate for her poor self-image, she admittedly fell for men she knew were no good for her, yet on whom she could depend to pay the bills. And then she would make snide remarks about her boyfriend's other woman who was where Margaret wanted to be.

Actually, I pointed out to Margaret that she needed to thank this woman for doing her the great favor of snatching her cheating man. If not for this "trashy" gal, Margaret would probably have remained entrenched in that disrespectful relationship indefinitely.

I instructed Margaret to learn to practice the following healing techniques:

1. Recognize that you are in total control of feeling better about yourself.
2. Vow that you will never again stay in a place where you feel shabby.
3. Eliminate blaming your childhood or your boyfriend for behavior you took on yourself.
4. Take full responsibility for where you are now and what you are about to do.

These are the keys to enhancing your self-worth, and you can follow them, too. But understand, once you do, there will be consequences to your being empowered.

Low self-worth is a popular excuse for staying in a place you know is bad for you. Actually, every advertising campaign supports this awful "less-than" place. Messages boldly blare, "Do you want to get rid of your frizzy, or flat, or straight, or mousey-colored hair?

Do you want to get *more* hair? Do you want to lose those unwanted pounds? Do you want a better body? Do you want whiter teeth? Do you want to become prettier, richer, or less wrinkly? If any or all these things are your desire, then here's a product for you!" With these proclamations, allegedly, whoever is feeling even a pinch of dissatisfaction with what they have, can get a new model of themselves, presto, chango.

Of course, there are no advertisements that promote becoming wiser. Wisdom would mean discriminating between what you *want* and what you *need*. With wisdom, people would recognize that they need none of the above, and that their true peace of mind would come from feeling good about themselves *as they are*. That's self-worth at its best.

Self-worth is our life power, and it usually entails pulling away from the cultural mentality that puts us down. Self-worth establishes us as independent thinkers and doers. It's not the happily-ever-after fairy tale ending, because the worthy princess doesn't need to *ask* the prince for permission to exhale. She takes the power that is rightly hers, and methodically pursues her desires.

Dear Dr. Gilda,

I just finished reading your book, "Don't Bet on the Prince! How to Have the Man You Want by Betting on Yourself." It's become my personal Bible. And it's made me see a lot of the women I know in a different light. I now notice how they've handed over their power to men, one after another.

> *A woman I work with moved in with her*
> *boyfriend. She has three kids from a previous marriage,*
> *this man treats her like his child, and yet she says she*
> *"loves him," and saves $600 in rent by staying with him.*
> *Another woman I know is moving out of state with her*
> *military boyfriend at the end of the month. He has yet to*
> *propose, but she waits for him to "come correct."*
>
> *Another woman just had a baby with her*
> *boyfriend who just finished school and decided to "chill*
> *out" and draw unemployment, rather than get a job. He*
> *says he is entitled to the free payout, so she works two*
> *jobs to provide for the baby. All these women say*
> *they're unhappy, but they don't do anything about their*
> *situations. Thank you for writing this book, Dr. Gilda.*
> *Now, at least, I know what not to do so that I don't end*
> *up like them!!*
> *Daria*

Daria's friends never believed, and never
projected that they *deserved* better than what they had.
Why didn't they? Because they feared that if they spoke
up, their men would leave. Being abandoned and alone
is most people's greatest fear. The partners these
women attracted sensed this, and capitalized on it. In
reality, if these women had trumpeted their
empowerment, their guys certainly would have left
because their relationships had been founded on these
women's *dis*empowerment.

I wrote my doctoral thesis on female school paraprofessionals who left the welfare rolls to pursue college educations and become full time teachers. My research uncovered that the men with whom the women started their lives couldn't handle their women's achievements, and one after another, left the relationships.

This could seem like the downside of your own empowerment. BUT, would anyone who is emotionally healthy and evolved want to remain with a man who wants a "less-than" woman? Changes such as these occur for the best. But insecure women often put themselves under the category of "Too Fearful to Move On."

Do you have the guts to become empowered, and let the people around you deal with it, in whichever way they might? Yes, this takes guts!! And rest assured, no one is going to thank you for developing the courage to confront him or her. No one will be happy that you no longer ask permission for his or her approval. No one is going to celebrate your becoming financially independent. Can you handle the downside of self-worth, in exchange for enjoying the upside of YOU?

For sure, the way you *treat* yourself is communicated by the way you *project* yourself. And the way you project yourself sets the stage for how others treat you. You've got the ability to make your world wonderful if you decide to enact the starring role. Every show has a star, and since it's YOUR show now,

YOU can be that star. Make yourself an "It" Person, and lift the curtains. Star in your own commercial.

Yes, create a commercial about yourself that boasts about what you believe you deserve. Boasting is a behavior we are taught to avoid. In fact, if you're like most women, you probably learned to deny and dismiss positive feedback whenever you were lucky enough to get it. How do you deal with compliments? Do you dismiss them and diminish their importance with, "Oh, it was nothing," or "It's OK," or "This shirt? I bought it on sale for only $20"?

The next time you feel embarrassed about accepting a compliment, stop yourself in your minimizing tracks and say instead, "Thank you." If you don't begin accepting your strengths with pride, people will withhold the praise you truly deserve. Not that you *need* applause any longer to feel good about yourself; it's just nice to know you can appreciate it when it does come.

Of course, you don't want to turn anyone off by your boasting. So how do you go from denying your assets to accepting praise graciously? The trick is to trumpet your talents without blasting your listeners' hearing. In other words,

Gilda-Gram®
Project a strong shell using a soft sell.

Like the length of all our TV and radio commercials, all you need is 30 seconds. Although that doesn't seem like a lot of time, in truth, it is harder to do a 30-second sell than it is to make a one-hour presentation. In a mere 30 seconds, you can't beat around the bush, you can't waste words that don't count, and you can't embroider the truth. Yes, in a mere 30 seconds, you can only project your unique essence, those elements that make you different from others out there. This is the real expression of your soul, the genuine and authentic representation of who you are.

If you still feel uncomfortable at first, put on a mask of confidence and act "as if" you feel it. In truth, your nervous system cannot tell the difference between what is real and what is imagined. So fake it till you make it!

<u>Gilda-Gram®</u>
Eventually, a confident outer mask will morph into reality.

Now you're ready to:

<u>Star in Your Own Commercial</u>

Time the following presentation you make. In 30 seconds, hook your audience as you describe your best assets. On video or audio, sell your best traits by saying, "I am terrific because . . ." Have a friend or family member watch you, and give you honest feedback. Then candidly assess yourself.

Self-Discovery

1. How did you feel about this "shameless" self-promotion?

2. Was 30 seconds enough time for you? Too much?

This is a very difficult activity for a lot of people. Most presenters hate to say glowing things about themselves! Why do you think that is?

Perform this exercise often. The more you sell yourself, the more you will raise your Deserve Level. And the higher your Deserve Level is, the more comfortable you will be in stating your needs and wants. That old hope-filled movie, "Field of Dreams," showed that if we build it, "he will come." *But if you don't advertise, "he"—whoever "he" may be—will never even know you're out there!*

Asking for what you want is a skill that can be learned. Of course, your previous hurts make you cautious about revealing yourself and showing your vulnerability. And like everyone else on the planet, you also fear rejection and abandonment. Who doesn't?

But there's a great upside to mastering this skill: when you're willing to show whom you really are, you'll attract Will-Be Winners like yourself. (And frankly, aren't you a bit fed up with all the Wanna-Be

Losers you've been hooking?) This is your chance at a new you, and a new kind of friends and lovers!!

Gilda-Gram®
We attract not whom we want,
but who we are.

You've got the power to make your life better. With sturdy self-worth, you attract winners because you deserve them. You deserve them because you know your power. You know your power because you are comfortable projecting who you are. Finally, you can display your specialness—without apology!!

Now there's just one more thing. And it's an ironic truism, the most surprising upside of self-esteem. So I purposely saved it for last. In fact, it is self-esteem's greatest power payoff of all:

Gilda-Gram®
When you have self-worth, you need not ask for
much. People automatically give to you!!

I know, I know, this book is called, "Ask for What You Want, AND GET IT!" But, as you now know, life is filled with paradoxes, and here's just one last one.

With strong self-worth, your entire body, attitude, and stance radiate your Deserve Level. **People will therefore give to you because you're YOU. If you have diligently followed all these suggestions, after all is said and done, you won't even have to bother asking for anything!**

Maybe I should have called this book, "*Don't Ask for What You Want, and Get It Anyway!*," because that's what will happen when you master these skills. And that's the wish I send you. Feel good about your inner strength, project it proudly, and others will feel it and share the goodness they have. Please let me know how it works for you!
Love,
Dr. Gilda

***

**Benefit from
Dr. Gilda's Personal Advice & Coaching
www.DrGilda.com**

***

MORE BOOKS BY DR. GILDA

Dr. Gilda's Relationship Series
--8 Steps to a Sizzling Marriage
--8 Tips to Understand the Opposite Sex

--10 Questions Single Women Should Never Ask
       & 10 They Should
--10 Signs of a Cheater-to-Be

Dr. Gilda's Self-Worth Series
-- I'm Worth Loving! Here's Why.
--Ask for What You Want—AND GET IT!
--How to Be a Worry-Free Woman

Dr. Gilda's Fidelity Series
--Why Your Cheater Keeps Cheating—And You're
    Still There!
--How to Cope with the Cheater You Love—and WIN
--99 Prescriptions for Fidelity: *Your Rx for Trust*

ALSO
--Don't Bet on the Prince! *How to Have the Man You*
    Want by Betting on Yourself
--Don't Lie on Your Back for a Guy Who Doesn't
    Have Yours

***

Dr. Gilda Carle (Ph.D.) is an internationally known media personality and relationship expert. She has authored 15 books, including "Don't Bet on the Prince!" (a test question on "Jeopardy!"), "Teen Talk with Dr. Gilda," "He's Not All That!," "How to WIN When Your Mate Cheats" (winner of The London Book Festival literary award), "99 Prescriptions for Fidelity," and more. She also wrote the weekly "30-Second Therapist" column for the Today Show, and the "Ask

Dr. Gilda" advice columnist for Match.com.

On TV, Dr. Gilda was the regular therapist for the Sally Jessy Raphael show, the "Love Doc" for MTV Online, and the TV host of "The Dr. Gilda Show" pilot for Twentieth Century Fox. In addition, she was the therapist in HBO's Emmy Award winner, "Telling Nicholas," featured on Oprah, where she guided a family to tell their 7-year-old that his mom died in the World Trade Center bombing.

In the corporate sector and in academia, she has her own management consulting firm, she is Professor Emerita, and she is a motivational speaker and a product spokesperson for such brands as Harlequin Books, Hallmark Cards, Cottonelle, Galderma Pharmaceuticals, Match.com, and more.

As President of Country Cures, Inc., her non-profit 501(c)(3) educational charity, she is the "Country Music Doctor." The organization uniquely uses Country Music to re-build the relationships of re-entering veterans and their families. If you, or someone you know, can benefit from this help, please visit **www.CountryCures.org**.

Reach Dr. Gilda at
www.DrGilda.com
or
www.CountryCures.org